AI Brain-Computer Interfaces & Neurotech

How Technology Connects Directly to the Human Mind

By Joe Correa

Published by Live Stronger Faster

This book is for educational and informational purposes only. The author and publisher are not engaged in rendering legal, financial, or other professional advice. Readers should consult a qualified professional before making any financial decisions.

First Edition

Table of Contents

Introduction

For centuries, the human brain has been the most powerful, mysterious, and untouchable system known to science. Every tool humanity has ever built—from language and mathematics to machines and medicine—has been an external extension of thought, never a direct connection to it. Until now. We are entering an era in which technology no longer merely responds to human input but interfaces with the brain itself. Brain-computer interfaces (BCIs), neural implants, wearable neurotech, and AI-driven signal decoding systems are dissolving the boundary between mind and machine. This book exists at the intersection of neuroscience, artificial intelligence, and human potential—where thoughts can be read, intention can be translated into action, and damaged neural pathways can be bypassed, repaired, or enhanced. What was once the domain of science fiction is now moving rapidly into clinical trials, consumer technology, and everyday life.

Brain-computer interfaces represent one of the most profound technological shifts in human history because they do not simply enhance the body or the environment—they directly engage with cognition itself. By translating neural signals into digital data and feeding information back into the brain, BCIs allow AI systems to learn how the brain communicates, adapts, and heals. This creates a two-way dialogue between biological intelligence and artificial intelligence. In recovery settings, BCIs already allow paralyzed patients to move robotic limbs, type with thought alone, or retrain damaged brain regions after injury. In performance and longevity contexts, neurotech is being explored to improve attention, accelerate learning, regulate emotions, and preserve cognitive function as the brain ages. The implications are not incremental—they are transformational.

At the core of this revolution is neuroplasticity, the brain's lifelong ability to reorganize itself. AI does not replace this natural capability; it amplifies it. Brain-computer interfaces give neuroplasticity feedback at a speed and precision the brain has never experienced before. Instead of relying solely on trial and error, repetition, or passive rehabilitation, AI-powered neurotech provides real-time insight into what the brain is doing, which neural circuits are firing, and how efficiently signals are traveling. This feedback allows the brain to correct itself faster, build stronger pathways, and recover functions that were once considered permanently lost. In this sense, BCIs are not external devices—they become training partners for the brain itself.

This book approaches brain-computer interfaces not as distant, abstract innovations, but as practical tools that are already reshaping medicine, rehabilitation, communication, and human performance. You will explore how neural signals are captured, interpreted, and enhanced using AI; how invasive and non-invasive neurotechnologies differ; and how machine learning models adapt to the unique neural patterns of each individual brain. More importantly, you will understand why these technologies matter—not just for people with neurological injuries or disabilities, but for anyone interested in cognitive health, resilience, and long-term mental clarity. The future of brain-computer interfaces is not limited to restoring what was lost; it is about expanding what is possible.

Ethical considerations are inseparable from this conversation. When technology can read intention, influence attention, or stimulate specific brain regions, questions of autonomy, consent, privacy, and identity become unavoidable. This book does not shy away from those realities. Instead, it provides a grounded framework for understanding how neurotech can be developed and used responsibly. AI systems trained on neural data must be designed with transparency, security, and human agency at the center. The goal is not control over the mind, but collaboration with it. Neurotechnology should empower individuals to heal, learn, and thrive—not reduce the human experience to a set of exploitable signals. Throughout this introduction and the chapters that follow, you will see how brain-computer interfaces fit naturally within the broader arc of AI-assisted brain healing explored in the earlier books of this series. Emotional regulation, memory optimization, sleep recovery, and behavioral change all converge here. BCIs provide a direct channel through which many of those systems can operate with greater precision and personalization. When AI understands the language of the brain, interventions no longer rely on guesswork. Therapy becomes adaptive. Rehabilitation becomes measurable. Mental training becomes individualized. The brain is no longer treated as a black box—it becomes an active participant in its own optimization.

This book is written for a wide audience: clinicians seeking to understand emerging tools, technologists building the next generation of neurotech, and individuals who want to stay informed about how AI is reshaping the human experience. You do not need a background in neuroscience or engineering to engage with these ideas. Concepts are explained clearly, with a focus on real-world applications and future trajectories rather than technical abstraction. The aim is comprehension, not intimidation—empowerment, not speculation. By the end of this book, you will be able to evaluate neurotechnology claims critically, understand where the field is headed, and make informed decisions about its role in your life or work.

We are living through a moment when the brain is no longer the final frontier—it is the next interface. AI-powered neurotechnology is redefining how humans recover from injury, adapt to stress, extend cognitive lifespan, and interact with the digital world. This shift will influence medicine, education, work, creativity, and even how we define intelligence itself. Book 7 of this series invites you to step inside that transformation. Not as a passive observer, but as a conscious participant in the era where human minds and intelligent machines evolve together.

Chapter 1

The Birth of the Brain–Machine Connection

The story of brain-computer interfaces begins with a simple but radical question: what if the electrical language of the brain could be translated into action without passing through muscles, speech, or movement? For most of human history, the brain's signals were locked inside the skull, observable only through behavior or injury. Neuroscience could infer function, but it could not converse with cognition. The emergence of brain-computer interfaces changed that relationship entirely. By capturing neural activity directly and using artificial intelligence to decode its patterns, scientists discovered that thought itself could become a usable signal. This chapter explores how that breakthrough occurred, why AI was essential to it, and how the brain learned—remarkably fast—to cooperate with machines.

Early experiments in neurotechnology relied on crude electrodes and simplistic signal processing. Researchers could detect spikes of electrical activity, but meaning was elusive. The brain does not operate with a single signal or predictable pathway; it communicates through distributed networks, oscillations, and probabilities. Traditional software struggled to interpret this complexity. The arrival of machine learning altered the equation. Instead of forcing neural data into rigid models, AI systems learned from the data itself. They identified recurring patterns, adapted to noise, and improved through feedback. This was the moment when brain-computer interfaces moved from laboratory curiosity to viable technology. AI did not merely analyze the brain—it learned its dialect.

One of the most important discoveries was that the brain adapts to interfaces as much as interfaces adapt to the brain. When neural signals were linked to external outcomes—moving a cursor, activating a robotic limb, selecting letters on a screen—the brain began to reorganize itself around the task. New neural pathways formed. Signal clarity improved. Control became smoother. This phenomenon revealed a powerful truth: brain-computer interfaces are not static tools but dynamic training environments for neuroplasticity. AI accelerates this process by continuously refining how signals are interpreted, reducing cognitive load, and reinforcing successful neural strategies. The interface becomes an extension of the nervous system rather than a foreign device.

As BCIs evolved, two primary approaches emerged: invasive and non-invasive systems. Invasive interfaces, implanted directly into brain tissue, offer high-resolution signals and precise control but carry surgical risk. Non-invasive systems, such as EEG-based headsets, prioritize safety and accessibility while relying heavily on AI to compensate for weaker signals. In both cases, artificial intelligence is the deciding factor. Without adaptive algorithms, neural data is too noisy and individualized to be useful. With AI, even subtle patterns become actionable. This democratizes neurotechnology, allowing more people to benefit from brain-machine communication without medical intervention.

The instructional importance of this chapter lies in understanding that BCIs are not mind-reading devices in the mythical sense. They do not extract thoughts, memories, or identity. Instead, they detect intention, attention, and neural states associated with specific tasks. AI learns correlations, not consciousness. This distinction matters because it reframes fear into function. The technology does not override free will; it depends on it. A brain-computer interface only works when the user engages, focuses, and learns. In this way, BCIs reinforce agency rather than diminish it.

Clinical applications provide the clearest evidence of this partnership. Stroke survivors use BCIs to retrain motor pathways by imagining movement while AI-driven systems stimulate correct neural circuits. Patients with spinal cord injuries regain functional independence by controlling assistive devices through intention alone. Individuals with communication disorders type and speak through neural signals when speech muscles fail. In each case, the brain is not bypassed—it is rehabilitated. AI provides structure and feedback, while neuroplasticity does the healing work.

Beyond recovery, BCIs are entering performance and wellness domains. Researchers are exploring how neural feedback can optimize focus, regulate stress, and enhance learning speed. AI monitors brain states and adjusts stimulation, tasks, or environments in real time. This creates closed-loop systems in which the brain receives immediate feedback about its own functioning. Such loops are powerful because the brain is inherently predictive; when given accurate feedback, it rapidly improves efficiency. Over time, skills internalize, and reliance on the interface decreases—a sign of successful neural adaptation rather than dependency.

Ethical and developmental considerations shape the future of this field. As brain-machine connections become more common, standards for data privacy, consent, and transparency must evolve. Neural data is deeply personal, yet it is also highly contextual and task-specific. This chapter emphasizes that responsible neurotechnology focuses on empowerment, reversibility, and user control. AI models must be auditable and aligned with human values. The goal is not permanent integration at all costs, but optional augmentation where benefits clearly outweigh risks.

The birth of brain-computer interfaces marks a turning point in human evolution—not because machines become dominant, but because humans gain new ways to communicate with themselves. AI acts as a translator, mediator, and accelerator, enabling the brain to observe, refine, and extend its own capabilities. As you move forward in this book, remember that neurotechnology is not about replacing cognition. It is about revealing its flexibility. The brain has always been adaptive. AI simply gave it a mirror and a faster feedback loop.

The Signal That Learned to Listen

Elena first noticed the silence before she noticed the loss. Her right hand lay still on the hospital blanket, obedient but absent, as if it belonged to someone else. The stroke had arrived without warning, a brief interruption that fractured her body's communication with itself. Doctors spoke gently about recovery windows and rehabilitation plans, but what Elena felt most was distance—between intention and action, thought and result. She could imagine movement vividly, yet nothing followed. It was as though her mind was speaking into a void.

Weeks later, a technician placed a lightweight headset over her scalp and explained that the system would listen, not command. Elena was skeptical. She had spent months being told what she could not do. The idea that a machine might understand her better than her own body felt absurd. Still, she agreed. On the screen in front of her, a small dot waited. The instruction was simple: imagine moving your hand. No pressure, no force—just intention. The dot flickered. Barely. But it moved.

At first, the connection was fragile. Some days the dot responded; other days it drifted aimlessly. The AI adjusted silently in the background, learning Elena's neural rhythms, filtering noise, recognizing patterns she could not consciously feel. Each session felt less like therapy and more like conversation. When Elena focused, the system responded. When she tired, it softened the task. She began to sense that something was listening—not judging, not correcting, simply adapting.

As weeks passed, something unexpected happened. Elena's hand twitched. Just once, involuntarily, but undeniably hers. The therapists celebrated, but Elena felt something deeper: recognition. Her brain was finding new routes, rerouting messages through pathways that had been dormant or forgotten. The interface did not force this change. It invited it. The AI learned from her, and she learned from herself.

One afternoon, Elena removed the headset and tried the exercise alone. She imagined movement, just as before. Her fingers lifted slightly, then settled. It was imperfect, slow, but real. The machine was no longer necessary in that moment. It had served its purpose as a bridge. Elena understood then that the technology had not healed her—it had taught her brain how to heal itself.

Months later, Elena returned to the lab, not as a patient but as a volunteer mentor. She watched others struggle with the same disbelief she once felt. She told them what no brochure could explain: that the interface was not reading their minds, but listening patiently until the brain remembered how to speak. In that quiet exchange between neuron and algorithm, Elena had found something more than recovery. She had rediscovered trust—in her mind's ability to adapt, and in technology's potential to serve without taking over.

The signal had learned to listen, and in doing so, it reminded the brain of its own resilience.

Chapter 2

Decoding Thought: How AI Translates Neural Signals into Action

The greatest challenge in brain-computer interface development has never been signal capture—it has been interpretation. The human brain generates immense volumes of electrical and chemical activity every second, most of it unrelated to conscious intention. Early neurotechnology could detect these signals, but without context they were little more than noise. Chapter 2 examines how artificial intelligence became the missing link that transformed raw neural activity into meaningful, actionable output. This transformation did not happen through better hardware alone, but through learning systems capable of adapting to the brain's variability, complexity, and individuality.

Neural signals are probabilistic, not deterministic. A single thought does not produce a single, repeatable waveform. Instead, intention emerges from patterns across populations of neurons, shaped by mood, fatigue, environment, and prior learning. Traditional rule-based software failed because it expected consistency where none existed. AI succeeded because it embraced variability. Machine learning models do not require predefined rules; they discover relationships by exposure. When applied to neural data, these systems learn which patterns correspond to attention, movement planning, relaxation, or effort. Over time, the model becomes fluent in the user's neural "accent," adjusting to shifts in brain state rather than resisting them.

This decoding process is iterative and reciprocal. In early sessions, AI models make imperfect predictions, and the user experiences inconsistent control. However, the brain responds to feedback faster than most technologies anticipate. When an intended action succeeds—even partially—the brain reinforces the neural pathways that produced it. When it fails, alternative pathways are explored. AI tracks these changes, updating its internal models in near real time. This creates a feedback loop in which both biological and artificial systems learn simultaneously. Control improves not because one side dominates, but because both adapt.

An important instructional insight is that decoding does not require invasive access to the brain's deepest structures to be effective. Non-invasive BCIs rely on surface-level signals that reflect aggregated neural activity. While less precise, these signals still contain rich information when interpreted with advanced AI. Deep learning architectures, temporal pattern recognition, and adaptive filtering allow algorithms to extract intention from subtle changes in frequency, timing, and synchronization. This means meaningful brain-machine interaction can occur without surgery, making neurotechnology accessible beyond clinical extremes.

Contextual awareness further enhances decoding accuracy. Modern AI-driven BCIs do not analyze neural signals in isolation; they integrate contextual data such as task demands, prior performance, environmental cues, and physiological signals like heart rate or eye movement. This multimodal approach mirrors how the brain itself operates—by integrating information rather than relying on a single input. As context improves, decoding becomes less cognitively demanding for the user. The system anticipates intention instead of reacting to it, reducing effort and increasing fluidity.

Crucially, AI does not decode "thoughts" in a narrative or semantic sense. It decodes states and intentions associated with specific tasks. This distinction protects cognitive privacy while enabling functionality. The system cannot know what a person is thinking about philosophically or emotionally unless it is explicitly trained for a related task. Even then, outputs are constrained to predefined actions or feedback mechanisms. Understanding this boundary is essential for ethical deployment and public trust. Learning curves vary widely among users, and AI accommodates this diversity. Some brains establish control quickly, while others require extended training. Rather than labeling users as capable or incapable, AI systems adjust difficulty, sensitivity, and feedback timing to meet the brain where it is. This adaptive scaffolding mirrors effective human teaching. As competence grows, assistance fades. Successful decoding is therefore measured not by dependency, but by how well the brain internalizes the skill.

As decoding accuracy improves, the interface becomes less visible to the user. Control feels intuitive rather than deliberate. At this stage, the brain is no longer translating intention consciously—it is acting. This is the ultimate goal of brain-computer interfaces: seamless integration without intrusion. AI's role is to fade into the background, leaving behind enhanced neural pathways and restored confidence. The technology succeeds when it becomes unnecessary.

Chapter 2 establishes that decoding neural signals is not an act of extraction, but of collaboration. AI does not steal meaning from the brain; it co-creates it through feedback, adaptation, and respect for biological limits. This understanding reframes neurotechnology as a learning partnership rather than a control system. With decoding in place, the foundation is set for more advanced applications explored in later chapters—closed-loop stimulation, augmentation, and long-term cognitive preservation.

Learning the Language Between

Marcus had always been quick with his hands. As a mechanical engineer, he trusted motion more than words. When a spinal injury severed the connection between his brain and his lower body, the silence that followed was unbearable. His thoughts remained sharp, his intentions intact, yet action had become theoretical. When he was offered a trial involving a brain-computer interface, Marcus agreed—not because he believed it would work, but because he needed something to engage with, something that still responded.

The first sessions were frustrating. The cursor on the screen jittered unpredictably, sometimes obeying, sometimes defying him entirely. Marcus blamed himself at first, assuming he was "thinking wrong." The researchers corrected him gently. There was no wrong way, they explained. The system was learning. So was he. The idea unsettled Marcus. He was used to mastering tools, not negotiating with them.

Over time, subtle changes emerged. When Marcus relaxed his jaw and softened his focus, the cursor steadied. When he strained, it wandered. The AI adjusted silently, filtering out noise, weighting certain patterns more heavily. Marcus began to sense a rhythm—not in the machine, but in himself. He was learning how his own intention felt before it became movement. Weeks later, Marcus controlled a robotic arm for the first time. The motion was slow, but unmistakable. He reached, grasped, and released. Each success felt less like operating equipment and more like reclaiming a conversation his body had forgotten how to hold. The AI did not command the arm; it anticipated him. When he hesitated, it waited. When he committed, it followed.

One afternoon, the system malfunctioned briefly, forcing a reset. Marcus sat still, waiting, and noticed something surprising: the effort he had once needed to concentrate was gone. The intention felt cleaner, more direct. The machine returned online, and control resumed instantly. The learning had already happened—inside him.

Marcus later described the experience not as being decoded, but as being understood. The interface had learned the space between his thoughts and actions, and in doing so, helped him bridge it himself. The language between brain and machine was not binary or mechanical. It was adaptive, patient, and deeply human.

Chapter 3

Closed-Loop Neurotechnology: When the Brain Talks Back

The evolution of brain-computer interfaces reaches a critical threshold when communication becomes bidirectional. Early systems focused on one-way decoding—extracting neural signals and translating them into external actions. While powerful, this approach only leveraged half of the brain's adaptive potential. Closed-loop neurotechnology completes the circuit. In these systems, artificial intelligence not only interprets brain activity but responds to it in real time through feedback, stimulation, or environmental adjustment. This chapter explores how closed-loop BCIs transform neurotechnology from a control interface into a self-correcting, self-optimizing learning system for the brain.

Closed-loop systems are grounded in a simple biological truth: the brain learns fastest when feedback is immediate, relevant, and precise. In natural settings, this feedback comes from sensory input, social cues, and physical consequences. Injury, illness, or chronic stress often disrupts these loops, slowing recovery and distorting perception. AI-powered neurotechnology restores and enhances feedback pathways by monitoring neural states continuously and delivering targeted responses. These responses may take the form of visual cues, auditory signals, haptic feedback, or direct neural stimulation, depending on the system. The key is timing. Feedback delivered within milliseconds can reshape neural pathways far more efficiently than delayed intervention.

Artificial intelligence is essential because closed-loop systems must adapt dynamically. The brain is not static; its optimal states shift with fatigue, emotion, circadian rhythms, and learning progress. Fixed feedback rules fail quickly under such variability. AI models track patterns over time, learning when to intervene, when to withdraw, and how strongly to respond. In rehabilitation, this allows stimulation to be synchronized with intention, reinforcing correct neural firing rather than overwhelming the system. In performance training, it enables fine-tuned optimization without overtraining or burnout. The loop remains flexible, responsive, and individualized.

One of the most significant applications of closed-loop neurotechnology is neural rehabilitation. After stroke or traumatic brain injury, damaged circuits often misfire or remain silent. Traditional therapy relies on repetition and hope that plasticity will eventually compensate. Closed-loop BCIs accelerate this process by detecting when the brain attempts a correct action and immediately reinforcing that attempt through stimulation or feedback. Even when physical movement is impossible, imagined movement paired with AI-timed feedback strengthens motor pathways. Over time, the brain relearns how to communicate with the body, often faster than with passive therapy alone.

Closed-loop systems also play a growing role in emotional regulation and mental health. Stress, anxiety, and depression are associated with identifiable neural patterns and dysregulated feedback loops. AI-driven neurotech can detect these patterns and guide the brain back toward stability through breathing cues, adaptive soundscapes, or neuromodulation. Importantly, the system does not impose calm—it teaches the brain how to return to it. With repeated exposure, users internalize regulation skills, reducing dependence on the technology. The loop trains resilience rather than replacing it.

From an instructional standpoint, it is crucial to understand that closed-loop neurotechnology is not constant stimulation. Effective systems intervene minimally, only when beneficial. Overstimulation can blunt neuroplasticity or create reliance. AI models are therefore trained to recognize diminishing returns and back off accordingly. This mirrors good coaching: guidance is strongest at the beginning and fades as mastery develops. The success of a closed-loop system is measured by how well it disappears over time. Ethical design becomes even more critical in closed-loop contexts. When technology can influence neural activity directly, safeguards must ensure user autonomy and informed consent. Closed-loop systems should be transparent, adjustable, and reversible. Users must understand when and how feedback is delivered, and retain the ability to disengage. This chapter emphasizes that responsible neurotechnology respects the brain's sovereignty. AI is a guide, not a governor.

Closed-loop neurotechnology represents a shift from reactive to participatory healing and enhancement. The brain is no longer treated as a passive recipient of intervention, but as an active collaborator. AI listens, responds, and adapts, while the brain experiments, learns, and refines. This partnership unlocks levels of recovery and performance previously unattainable through one-way systems. With closed loops in place, neurotechnology becomes less about machinery and more about dialogue.

As this chapter concludes, it becomes clear that the future of brain-computer interfaces lies not in stronger signals or faster processors alone, but in better conversations between mind and machine. Closed-loop systems embody that conversation. They transform AI from an external observer into an adaptive partner in neuroplastic change, setting the stage for deeper integration, longer cognitive lifespan, and more personalized brain health explored in the chapters ahead.

The Quiet Return

Lina had forgotten what calm felt like. Years of chronic anxiety had trained her nervous system to expect threat everywhere—in silence, in crowds, even in rest. Therapy had helped her understand her patterns, but understanding did not always translate into relief. When she enrolled in a neurofeedback program using AI-driven closed-loop technology, she did not expect transformation. She hoped only for moments of quiet.

The system was simple. Sensors monitored her brain activity while she listened to a gentle soundscape. The AI adjusted the tones in response to her neural state, subtly shifting pitch and rhythm as her brain drifted toward or away from regulation. At first, Lina noticed nothing. The sounds washed over her like background noise. But after several sessions, she began to feel something unfamiliar—a pause between thoughts.

When her anxiety spiked, the soundscape tightened, becoming sharper, almost urging her attention inward. When she relaxed, the tones softened. There was no instruction, no command to "calm down." The system responded, and her brain followed. Slowly, Lina learned the sensation of balance—not as an idea, but as a physical state.

One evening, the system paused unexpectedly due to a software update. Lina sat in the quiet room, waiting. Minutes passed. She realized her breath was steady. Her shoulders were loose. The feedback loop was gone, but the calm remained. The technology had not given her peace—it had taught her how to recognize it.

Weeks later, Lina no longer needed daily sessions. She used the system occasionally, as a reminder rather than a crutch. In moments of stress, she could summon the same internal signals the AI once mirrored back to her. The loop had closed, then opened again, leaving her with something enduring.

Lina described the experience as a conversation that gradually faded into intuition. The machine listened when she could not. Eventually, she learned to listen to herself. In that quiet return, she found not dependence on technology, but independence from fear.

Chapter 4

Neural Augmentation & Cognitive Enhancement

Once brain-computer interfaces moved beyond restoration and into reliable communication and feedback, a new frontier emerged: augmentation. Neural augmentation does not aim to fix what is broken, but to expand what already works. This distinction is critical. Augmentation reframes neurotechnology from a medical intervention into a cognitive tool, one that partners with the brain to improve focus, learning speed, memory retention, and mental endurance. Chapter 4 explores how AI-driven neurotech enhances human capability without replacing natural cognition, and why augmentation depends more on training and feedback than on raw stimulation.

Cognitive performance has always been limited by bandwidth. Attention fluctuates, memory decays, and mental fatigue accumulates. Traditional methods—education, practice, mindfulness—improve performance indirectly, often slowly. AI neurotechnology accelerates these processes by making internal brain states visible and trainable. When the brain receives precise feedback about attention quality, cognitive load, or fatigue thresholds, it adjusts rapidly. AI models detect subtle neural signatures associated with optimal performance states and guide users back toward them, reinforcing efficiency rather than forcing effort.

Attention enhancement is one of the earliest and most practical applications of neural augmentation. Focus is not a constant state but a dynamic balance between engagement and rest. AI-driven BCIs monitor neural rhythms associated with sustained attention and mind-wandering, adjusting tasks or environments in real time. Rather than demanding constant concentration, these systems teach the brain how to enter focus more quickly and exit it cleanly. Over time, users develop greater control over attentional shifts, reducing burnout and improving productivity without increasing cognitive strain.

Memory augmentation follows a similar principle. Memory formation depends on timing, emotional relevance, and neural synchronization. AI systems trained on neural data can identify when the brain is most receptive to encoding new information and adjust learning conditions accordingly. This may involve pacing content, introducing brief pauses, or providing reinforcement at optimal moments. Importantly, augmentation does not store memories externally or bypass biological processes. It enhances the brain's natural encoding mechanisms, improving retention through alignment rather than substitution. Skill acquisition also benefits from neural augmentation. Complex skills—such as language learning, musical performance, or strategic reasoning—require coordinated activation across multiple brain regions. AI neurotech monitors these patterns and provides feedback that helps the brain refine them more efficiently. Instead of practicing blindly, learners receive insight into how their brain is engaging with the task. This shortens learning curves and reduces frustration, making mastery more accessible without diminishing the value of effort.

A key instructional concept in augmentation is non-invasiveness. Most cognitive enhancement applications rely on wearable or environmental neurotech rather than implants. This ensures reversibility and minimizes risk. AI compensates for lower signal resolution through adaptive modeling, allowing meaningful augmentation without permanent alteration. The brain remains in control. The technology supports, guides, and then recedes as skills internalize.

Ethical boundaries are especially important in augmentation contexts. Enhancing cognition raises questions about fairness, consent, and identity. This chapter emphasizes that augmentation should remain optional, transparent, and user-directed. AI systems must be designed to enhance well-being rather than enforce productivity or conformity. The goal is expanded agency, not optimization at any cost.

Augmentation succeeds when individuals feel more capable, not pressured.

Long-term studies suggest that well-designed augmentation does not create dependency. Instead, it accelerates learning until the brain no longer requires external feedback. As neural pathways strengthen, reliance decreases. This mirrors physical training: equipment supports development, but strength ultimately resides in the body. Neural augmentation works best when it leaves the brain stronger than it found it.

Chapter 4 positions AI neurotechnology as a catalyst for human potential rather than a replacement for human effort. Augmentation is not about becoming something other than human. It is about becoming more fully human—more attentive, more adaptable, and more capable of sustained thought in an increasingly complex world. With responsible design and informed use, neural augmentation becomes a tool for longevity of mind as much as performance of mind.

The Edge of Focus

Daniel had always prided himself on discipline. As a graduate student in theoretical physics, he believed focus was a moral trait—something earned through willpower alone. But as the work grew more abstract and demanding, his concentration began to fracture. Hours slipped by in mental fog. Reading the same paragraph repeatedly felt like pushing against glass. When his advisor suggested a cognitive training program using AI neurotechnology, Daniel resisted. He did not want shortcuts.

The system did not feel like a shortcut. It felt like a mirror. Wearing a lightweight neural band during study sessions, Daniel received subtle feedback—changes in screen lighting, pacing adjustments, brief pauses—based on his attentional state. At first, he found it distracting. Then he noticed a pattern. His mind wandered before he consciously realized it. The system responded faster than his awareness.

Over time, Daniel began to anticipate the feedback. He sensed the moment focus slipped, the precise instant effort turned into strain. The AI adjusted less frequently as his brain learned to self-correct. What surprised him most was not improved productivity, but reduced exhaustion. He was thinking deeply without fighting himself.

One afternoon, the system malfunctioned and shut down mid-session. Daniel continued working. The clarity remained. He finished a proof that had stalled for weeks, not with intensity, but with calm persistence. The technology had already done its work.

Months later, Daniel no longer used the system regularly. He had internalized the rhythm it taught him—the rise, sustain, and release of focus. He realized then that augmentation had not replaced discipline. It had refined it. The edge of focus was no longer something he chased. It was something he understood.

Daniel later described the experience as learning the physics of his own mind. The AI had not made him smarter. It had made his thinking cleaner. And in that clarity, his work finally had room to breathe.

Chapter 5

Identity, Agency & Ethics in Brain–AI Integration

As brain-computer interfaces mature from experimental tools into scalable technologies, the most consequential questions are no longer technical. They are human. When AI systems can interpret neural signals, deliver feedback, and even modulate brain activity, issues of identity, agency, and ethics move from abstract philosophy into everyday decision-making. Chapter 5 examines these questions not as distant hypotheticals, but as practical considerations that must shape how neurotechnology is designed, deployed, and governed. The future of brain–AI integration will be defined less by what is possible than by what is permitted, protected, and chosen.

At the center of this discussion is agency—the individual's ability to initiate, control, and terminate interaction with neurotechnology. A brain-computer interface is only ethical if participation is voluntary, informed, and reversible. Unlike external tools, neurotech operates at the level of cognition itself. This proximity demands higher standards. Users must understand what data is collected, how it is processed, and how feedback or stimulation is delivered. Agency is preserved when the user remains the final authority, not the algorithm.

AI should support decision-making, not replace it.

Identity presents a more subtle challenge. The brain is not merely a processor; it is the seat of personality, values, and self-perception. When neurotechnology alters attention, emotional regulation, or cognitive performance, users may experience changes in how they relate to themselves. This does not mean identity is overwritten or manufactured, but it does require thoughtful framing. Enhancement can feel unsettling if it is perceived as artificial rather than earned. Ethical neurotech design emphasizes continuity of self. Changes should feel integrated, not imposed, reinforcing the sense that growth originates within the individual.

Data ethics form another critical layer. Neural data is uniquely sensitive—not because it reveals thoughts verbatim, but because it reflects patterns of attention, stress, and engagement that are deeply personal. Unlike biometric data such as fingerprints or facial scans, neural signals are dynamic and context-dependent. Ethical systems minimize data retention, anonymize aggressively, and restrict use to explicit purposes. Commercial exploitation of neural data without clear consent undermines trust and threatens long-term adoption. Chapter 5 stresses that safeguarding neural data is not merely a legal obligation, but a moral one.

Bias and accessibility also shape ethical outcomes. AI systems trained on limited populations may perform unevenly across age groups, cultures, or neurological profiles. This risks creating cognitive "haves" and "have-nots," where only certain users benefit fully from augmentation or rehabilitation. Ethical deployment requires diverse training data, continuous auditing, and adaptive personalization. Neurotechnology should reduce inequality in cognitive health, not amplify it. Inclusivity is not optional—it is foundational.

Another ethical dimension involves dependency and over-optimization. Closed-loop systems and augmentation tools are powerful precisely because they accelerate learning. But without safeguards, users may rely on them longer than necessary or push cognitive limits unsustainably. Ethical AI systems are designed to fade, not dominate. They encourage independence by gradually reducing intervention as skills internalize. This principle distinguishes supportive technology from coercive optimization.

Governance frameworks are beginning to emerge, but they lag behind innovation. Regulation must balance safety with flexibility, avoiding both stagnation and unchecked experimentation. Chapter 5 argues for adaptive governance models that evolve with technology, informed by interdisciplinary expertise spanning neuroscience, ethics, law, and lived user experience. Static rules cannot anticipate dynamic systems. Ongoing dialogue is essential.

Ultimately, ethical brain–AI integration rests on respect for the human mind as an end in itself, not a means to productivity or profit alone. Neurotechnology reaches its highest value when it enhances autonomy, resilience, and self-understanding. This chapter does not prescribe a single moral stance, but provides principles to guide decision-making as individuals, developers, and societies navigate this frontier. The question is not whether brains will connect to AI—they already are. The question is under whose terms, and to whose benefit.

The Choice That Remained

Aisha worked in policy, not technology. When she volunteered for a pilot program studying neural augmentation in high-stress professions, she approached it analytically. The system promised improved focus and emotional regulation during long negotiation sessions. She agreed, on one condition: she wanted full visibility into how it worked and the ability to stop at any time. The researchers agreed.

The first weeks were subtle. Aisha noticed less fatigue, more patience. During tense meetings, her thoughts stayed organized instead of spiraling. What unsettled her was not the improvement, but the ease. She wondered whether the calm was hers or borrowed. The question followed her home.

One evening, after a particularly successful negotiation, Aisha turned the system off before a follow-up call. She wanted to feel the difference. The conversation was harder. Emotions flared. She had to slow herself consciously. Yet she managed. The skills were still there—just less automatic. Relief washed over her. The technology had not replaced her judgment. It had trained it.

Over the following months, Aisha used the system selectively. She declined an update that increased intervention frequency, despite measurable performance gains. The choice surprised the researchers. Aisha explained simply that she valued effort alongside effectiveness. She wanted support, not substitution.

When the pilot concluded, participants were offered continued access. Some accepted eagerly. Others declined. Aisha took time to decide. In the end, she kept the option open but unused, knowing it was there if needed. That knowledge—choice without pressure—mattered more than the tool itself.

Years later, when Aisha helped draft ethical guidelines for emerging neurotechnology, she drew on that experience. The most important safeguard, she argued, was not technical at all.

It was the right to say yes, the right to say no, and the right to change one's mind. In a world where minds could connect to machines, that freedom remained the most human interface of all.

Chapter 6

Human–AI Symbiosis: The Long-Term Brain Partnership

As brain-computer interfaces and neurotechnology mature, the relationship between human cognition and artificial intelligence shifts from short-term interaction to long-term partnership. Chapter 6 explores this emerging symbiosis—not as a merger where one replaces the other, but as a co-evolutionary process in which both systems adapt over time. Human–AI symbiosis in neurotechnology is defined by continuity, learning, and mutual influence. The brain shapes the AI through its unique neural patterns, while the AI shapes the brain through feedback, optimization, and support. Understanding this relationship is essential for anticipating how neurotech will influence cognition across years and decades, not just sessions or clinical trials.

The brain is inherently plastic, but plasticity follows use. Long-term interaction with AI-driven neurotech subtly alters how the brain allocates attention, processes information, and responds to challenge. When designed responsibly, these changes are not distortions but refinements. The brain learns which states are efficient, which patterns lead to clarity, and which habits produce resilience. AI accelerates this learning by providing consistent feedback and adaptive environments. Over time, the brain internalizes these lessons, reducing reliance on the technology while retaining the benefits. Symbiosis succeeds when growth persists even in the absence of the tool.

From the AI perspective, long-term partnership requires restraint as much as intelligence. Systems must avoid rigid optimization that locks users into narrow performance profiles. Human cognition thrives on variability, rest, and exploration. AI models that learn alongside the brain must accommodate curiosity, creativity, and even inefficiency. Chapter 6 emphasizes that the healthiest symbiotic systems are those that evolve with the user's goals, life stages, and values. A student's cognitive needs differ from those of a recovering patient or an aging professional. Symbiosis demands adaptability across contexts and time.

One of the most promising aspects of long-term brain–AI partnership is cognitive preservation. As the brain ages, processing speed and memory retrieval often decline, not due to loss of intelligence but reduced efficiency and neural noise. AI-driven neurotech can help compensate by reinforcing optimal neural pathways, supporting attention regulation, and maintaining engagement in cognitively demanding activities. This does not halt aging, but it can slow decline and preserve functional independence. Importantly, the partnership respects the brain's dignity—it supports rather than substitutes cognition.

Symbiosis also reshapes how individuals relate to technology psychologically. When AI becomes a consistent cognitive partner rather than an external tool, trust and familiarity develop. This raises important design considerations. Systems must remain interpretable and predictable to avoid over-reliance or misplaced attribution of authority. Users should understand what the AI can and cannot do, preserving realistic expectations. Transparency sustains trust, while opacity erodes it. Long-term success depends on maintaining this balance.

Another dimension of symbiosis involves collective intelligence. As more individuals interact with neurotechnology, aggregated insights—appropriately anonymized—can inform better system design and broader understanding of brain function. However, Chapter 6 reiterates that collective benefit must never override individual rights. Symbiosis begins at the personal level. Each brain–AI partnership is unique, shaped by biology, experience, and intention. Ethical frameworks must protect this individuality even as systems scale.

Education and preparation play a crucial role in long-term integration. Users must be taught not only how to operate neurotechnology, but how to disengage from it gracefully. Symbiosis includes the ability to step back, reflect, and recalibrate. The healthiest partnerships are those that enhance self-awareness rather than obscure it. AI should help users understand their own minds more clearly, not outsource understanding entirely.

Ultimately, human–AI symbiosis in neurotechnology represents a new phase of cognitive evolution—one guided by choice rather than inevitability. The brain does not surrender its role as the primary agent of thought. Instead, it gains a collaborator that can accelerate learning, support resilience, and extend cognitive lifespan. Chapter 6 frames this partnership as an opportunity to redefine intelligence not as competition between human and machine, but as cooperation in service of human flourishing.

The Long Conversation

Noah had been using neural assistance longer than he could remember. What began as rehabilitation after a traumatic brain injury had gradually evolved into something quieter and more personal. The system no longer guided his movements or regulated his emotions overtly. It sat in the background of his life, adjusting lighting when his focus waned, suggesting pauses when fatigue crept in. Most days, Noah barely noticed it. What he noticed instead was himself. His thinking felt cleaner than it had before the accident. He caught cognitive slips early. He rested without guilt. Friends joked that he seemed unusually present, as though he listened with his whole mind. Noah wondered whether the technology deserved credit, or whether it had simply reminded him how to listen to himself again.

One afternoon, a system update failed, disabling the AI entirely. Noah expected frustration. Instead, he felt curiosity. He went about his day without assistance, observing his own rhythms. Some tasks felt harder. Others felt unchanged. The partnership, he realized, had already done its work. The habits remained.

When the system came back online, Noah chose a lighter configuration. He did not want optimization at every moment. He wanted space. The AI adapted, quietly recalibrating. It did not insist. It learned, as it always had, from his choices.

Years later, as neurotechnology became more common, people asked Noah whether he felt "augmented." He struggled to answer. He did not feel more than human. He felt more himself. The long conversation between his mind and the machine had not replaced his voice. It had helped him hear it more clearly.

In the end, Noah understood that symbiosis was not about permanence. It was about alignment. The AI had walked with him for a time, then stepped back. What remained was not dependence, but a deeper familiarity with his own mind. That, he believed, was the highest form of integration any technology could achieve.

Chapter 7

The Limits, Risks & Realities of Brain–AI Technology

As brain–computer interfaces and AI-driven neurotechnology advance, it becomes increasingly important to separate promise from projection. Chapter 7 addresses the limits, risks, and real-world constraints of brain–AI integration, not to diminish its potential, but to ground it in reality. Every transformative technology carries boundaries shaped by biology, engineering, ethics, and human psychology. Understanding these boundaries protects users from unrealistic expectations and ensures that neurotechnology develops as a sustainable tool rather than a speculative myth.

The first and most fundamental limit is biological. The human brain, while remarkably plastic, is not infinitely malleable. Neural change requires energy, rest, and time. AI can accelerate learning and recovery, but it cannot bypass biological constraints such as metabolic limits, sleep requirements, or the need for gradual adaptation. Overstimulation, excessive feedback, or constant optimization can backfire, leading to fatigue, diminished returns, or neural stress. Chapter 7 emphasizes that effective neurotechnology works *with* biological rhythms, not against them.

Signal quality also imposes practical constraints. Even the most advanced non-invasive neurotech captures only partial representations of neural activity. AI compensates for this through modeling and prediction, but interpretation is never perfect. Noise, environmental interference, emotional variability, and individual differences all affect accuracy. This means brain–AI systems operate probabilistically, not deterministically. They improve likelihoods, not guarantees. Recognizing this helps users interpret outcomes realistically and avoid over-attributing authority to algorithmic outputs.

Another important limitation involves generalization. Neurotechnology is highly personalized by necessity. What works for one brain may not work for another, and models trained on specific tasks or contexts do not automatically transfer across domains. A system optimized for attention training may not enhance creativity. A rehabilitation protocol effective for one injury may fail for another. AI excels at specialization, but this strength becomes a limitation when broad claims are made. Responsible deployment requires clear scope definitions and continuous recalibration.

Psychological risks must also be addressed. While most well-designed systems reduce dependency over time, poorly implemented neurotechnology can encourage over-reliance or identity confusion. Users may attribute success or failure to the technology rather than their own effort, weakening self-efficacy. Chapter 7 underscores the importance of framing neurotech as a training aid, not a replacement for agency. Language matters. Design matters. Expectations matter.

Privacy and security risks persist despite best practices. Neural data, even when anonymized, carries unique sensitivity. Data breaches, misuse, or unauthorized secondary applications could undermine trust and cause harm. Technical safeguards must be paired with legal and ethical protections. This chapter reinforces that trust is fragile in neurotechnology contexts, and once lost, difficult to regain. Transparency, minimal data retention, and user control are not optional features—they are survival requirements for the field.

There are also social and cultural limits. Widespread adoption of brain–AI tools may provoke resistance, fear, or moral concern, particularly when public understanding lags behind innovation. Misrepresentation in media and popular culture can amplify unrealistic hopes or dystopian anxieties. Chapter 7 argues that education and honest communication are as critical as technical progress. Neurotechnology must be introduced gradually, with room for societal adaptation and debate.

Importantly, acknowledging limits does not weaken the case for neurotechnology—it strengthens it. Technologies that promise everything invite disappointment and backlash. Technologies that define boundaries earn trust. AI-driven brain interfaces are most powerful when applied where they demonstrably help: recovery, learning acceleration, regulation, and cognitive preservation. They are not tools for mind reading, personality replacement, or instant genius.

Chapter 7 concludes by reframing limits as design guides rather than obstacles. Boundaries force clarity, discipline, and humility. They remind developers and users alike that the brain is not a machine to be optimized endlessly, but a living system to be supported. When neurotechnology respects this reality, it remains a force for empowerment rather than illusion. The future of brain–AI integration depends not on ignoring limits, but on honoring them.

The Day the System Was Wrong

Ethan trusted data more than intuition. As a performance consultant, he had built his career on metrics, optimization, and measurable outcomes. When he began using an advanced AI neurofeedback system, he embraced it fully. The system tracked focus, stress, and cognitive efficiency, offering recommendations throughout his day. His productivity soared—until it didn't. One morning, the system flagged Ethan as cognitively depleted and advised rest. Ethan felt sharp, energized, ready. He ignored the alert and pushed forward. The work flowed easily at first, but by afternoon his thoughts fragmented. Errors crept in. Frustration followed. That evening, Ethan reviewed the data and realized something unsettling: the system had been right, but not infallible. It had detected patterns he didn't consciously feel—but it hadn't known his context, his motivation, his intention to push for a reason.

The next week, the system misclassified a state of creative exploration as distraction and attempted to redirect him repeatedly. Ethan grew irritated. He turned the feedback down, then off entirely. For the first time since adopting the technology, he worked without guidance. The result was messy but inspired. The contrast forced reflection.

Ethan reactivated the system with modified settings. He treated its insights as input, not instruction. When recommendations aligned with his experience, he followed them. When they didn't, he chose differently. Over time, the partnership stabilized—not because the AI improved, but because Ethan reframed its role.

Months later, Ethan spoke at a conference about neurotechnology adoption. Instead of highlighting peak performance gains, he spoke about failure cases, false positives, and human judgment. The room grew quiet. He concluded simply that the most powerful feature of any brain–AI system was the ability to disagree with it.

That day marked a shift in how Ethan related to technology. He no longer sought perfection from it. He sought perspective. The system remained valuable—not because it was always right, but because it reminded him that intelligence, artificial or biological, is strongest when it knows its limits.

Chapter 8

Consciousness, Awareness & the Question of the Self

As brain–computer interfaces evolve beyond performance, rehabilitation, and augmentation, they inevitably approach a deeper domain: consciousness itself. Chapter 8 explores how AI-driven neurotechnology influences awareness, perception, and the subjective experience of being human. This chapter does not attempt to define consciousness conclusively—no technology or discipline can—but instead examines how interacting directly with neural states reshapes self-awareness, introspection, and the sense of agency. When the brain can observe itself with the assistance of AI, consciousness becomes not just something we experience, but something we can study, train, and refine.

Consciousness has traditionally been treated as emergent and opaque, accessible only through reflection or philosophy. Neurotechnology introduces a practical shift. By identifying neural correlates of awareness—patterns associated with attention, presence, emotional tone, and cognitive integration—AI systems provide real-time feedback on states that were previously invisible. This does not reduce consciousness to data; it creates a bridge between subjective experience and objective measurement. The result is a new form of self-observation, where individuals learn to recognize mental states with greater precision and less judgment.

One of the most profound effects of brain–AI interaction is the decoupling of awareness from reactivity. Many people live in a near-constant state of cognitive reflex, driven by stress, habit, and external stimulation. AI-guided neurofeedback helps individuals recognize when they are operating on autopilot versus when they are genuinely present. Over time, this distinction becomes intuitive. Consciousness expands not by adding content, but by reducing noise. The mind becomes quieter, not emptier—more spacious, not disengaged.

This process mirrors long-standing contemplative practices such as meditation and mindfulness, but with a critical difference: immediacy. Traditional practices rely on subjective insight that can take years to develop. AI-assisted neurotechnology accelerates this learning by reflecting mental states back to the user in real time. The brain learns faster when it can see itself clearly. Importantly, the technology does not generate awareness—it highlights it. The capacity was always there. AI simply sharpens perception.

Chapter 8 also addresses the fear that brain–AI interaction might dilute or fragment the self. In practice, well-designed systems tend to produce the opposite effect. As individuals gain finer control over attention and emotional regulation, they report a stronger sense of coherence and identity. When mental states become less overwhelming and more navigable, the self feels more stable, not less. Consciousness becomes something inhabited rather than endured.

However, this domain demands restraint. Consciousness is not a performance metric. Attempts to optimize awareness aggressively or force transcendence can destabilize mental health, particularly for vulnerable individuals. Ethical neurotechnology respects psychological boundaries and progresses gradually. AI systems must be designed to support integration, grounding, and reflection—not dissociation or overstimulation. This chapter emphasizes that depth of awareness grows best when paired with stability.

Another important theme is authorship of experience. When AI systems provide feedback on mental states, users may question whether insights originate from within or from the machine. Over time, effective systems dissolve this distinction. Feedback becomes redundant as awareness internalizes. The individual learns to recognize patterns without assistance. In this sense, AI acts as a temporary scaffold for consciousness, not a permanent interpreter. Chapter 8 reframes the relationship between technology and consciousness as educational rather than intrusive. The brain is not being observed by an external authority; it is learning to observe itself more skillfully. This reframing preserves dignity and autonomy. Consciousness remains personal, subjective, and irreducible, even as it becomes more intelligible.

This chapter concludes by proposing that the greatest contribution of brain–AI integration may not be enhanced productivity or longevity, but enhanced presence. In a world increasingly shaped by abstraction and acceleration, neurotechnology offers a way back into direct experience. Not by retreating from technology, but by using it to reconnect with the most fundamental interface of all: awareness itself.

Watching the Watcher

Maya had practiced meditation for years, though she rarely spoke about it. The practice had softened her reactions but left her with questions she couldn't articulate. When a research group invited her to participate in a study on AI-assisted awareness training, she hesitated. Meditation, to her, felt sacred—intimate. The idea of involving technology felt intrusive. Still, curiosity won.

The system did not instruct her to meditate. It simply mirrored her neural state through subtle visual feedback. When her mind wandered, the image fragmented. When she settled, it stabilized. There were no labels, no judgments. Just reflection. At first, Maya found it distracting. Then something shifted. She noticed the exact moment a thought formed, the precise instant attention drifted. The feedback arrived not as correction, but as confirmation.

During one session, the image remained steady for an extended period. Maya felt deeply present, but what surprised her was not the calm—it was the absence of effort. Awareness was simply there, watching itself. The system eventually faded the feedback automatically. The state remained.

In the weeks that followed, Maya practiced without the technology. She recognized the same internal cues, the same spaciousness. The AI had not taught her something new. It had shown her what she already knew, more clearly.

One evening, Maya sat quietly at home and realized she no longer needed to ask whether awareness belonged to her or the system. The question no longer made sense. The observer had always been present. The technology had simply pointed.

When the study concluded, Maya declined continued access. The researchers seemed surprised. She thanked them and explained that the work was complete. Consciousness, she had learned, was not something to improve. It was something to notice.

Years later, Maya would describe the experience as learning to watch the watcher. Not through effort, not through belief, but through clarity. The machine had left. What remained was presence—unchanged, uninterrupted, and undeniably her own.

Chapter 9

Longevity, Brain Aging & Cognitive Preservation

As humanity lives longer, the central challenge of aging shifts from extending years to preserving quality of mind within those years. Chapter 9 explores how AI-driven neurotechnology intersects with brain aging, cognitive decline, and long-term mental resilience. Unlike acute injury or short-term performance goals, longevity demands sustained support over decades. The objective is not to freeze the brain in youth, but to help it adapt gracefully to change, maintaining clarity, independence, and identity as time progresses. AI neurotechnology offers new tools for this challenge—not as a cure for aging, but as a companion to it.

Cognitive aging is often misunderstood as a uniform decline. In reality, different brain functions age at different rates. Vocabulary and pattern recognition may improve with experience, while processing speed, working memory, and attentional flexibility may gradually diminish. AI systems trained on longitudinal neural data can detect these shifts early, often before symptoms are noticeable. Early detection enables proactive intervention—adjusting cognitive load, reinforcing vulnerable pathways, and maintaining engagement in mentally demanding activities. Prevention, in this context, is more effective than remediation.

One of the most powerful contributions of AI neurotechnology to longevity is personalized cognitive maintenance. No two brains age the same way. Genetics, lifestyle, stress exposure, sleep quality, and intellectual engagement all influence trajectories. AI models adapt to these variables, learning an individual's baseline and tracking subtle deviations over time. This allows interventions to be tailored dynamically—strengthening memory circuits when they weaken, supporting attention when fatigue increases, and promoting rest when overstimulation threatens resilience.

Neuroplasticity remains active throughout life, but it requires encouragement. Without challenge, the brain conserves energy by narrowing activity. AI-guided neurotech counteracts this tendency by introducing adaptive complexity—tasks and feedback that are neither too easy nor overwhelming. This "just-right" stimulation keeps neural networks flexible and engaged. Over time, such engagement supports cognitive reserve, the brain's ability to compensate for age-related changes or pathology. Cognitive reserve does not prevent all decline, but it dramatically influences how well individuals function despite it. Sleep, stress regulation, and emotional stability play critical roles in brain aging, and AI neurotechnology integrates these domains rather than treating cognition in isolation. Closed-loop systems monitor neural markers of fatigue, dysregulation, and overload, guiding users toward restorative states. Chronic stress accelerates cognitive decline by impairing memory consolidation and increasing neural noise. By helping the brain return to balance more efficiently, AI systems indirectly protect long-term cognitive health.

Chapter 9 also addresses neurodegenerative conditions, where AI neurotechnology holds promise but requires humility. While current systems cannot reverse diseases such as Alzheimer's or Parkinson's, they may delay progression, support remaining function, and improve quality of life. AI-driven cognitive training, neural stimulation, and assistive interfaces can help individuals maintain autonomy longer. Importantly, these tools must be framed realistically to avoid false hope. Their value lies in support, not cure.

An essential ethical consideration in longevity-focused neurotechnology is dignity. Aging individuals must remain active participants in their care, not passive recipients of optimization. Systems should adapt to changing goals—prioritizing comfort, meaning, and connection alongside cognition. AI must respect the evolving priorities of the user, recognizing that what matters at 30 differs from what matters at 80. Longevity is not merely about preservation of function, but preservation of self.

This chapter also considers intergenerational impact. As neurotechnology becomes more common, future generations may inherit both improved tools and expanded expectations for cognitive health. This could reshape how societies view aging, shifting narratives from inevitable decline to supported adaptation. However, access and equity remain central concerns. Longevity technologies must not become privileges of a few. Inclusive design and public investment will determine whether cognitive preservation becomes a societal benefit or a source of inequality.

Chapter 9 concludes by reframing brain longevity as a relationship rather than a target. AI neurotechnology does not promise immortality of mind. It offers something more realistic and humane: the ability to stay engaged, present, and capable for as long as possible. By partnering with the brain's natural adaptability, AI helps aging become a process of transformation rather than loss. In this partnership, longevity is not measured solely in years lived, but in moments experienced with clarity and meaning.

The Last Notebook

Eleanor had always loved words. As a teacher, she filled notebooks with observations, quotes, and small reflections from her days in the classroom. When she retired, the habit remained. What changed was her memory. Names slipped away. Sentences dissolved mid-thought. At first, she laughed it off. Then she began writing reminders to herself.

When her daughter suggested a cognitive support program using AI neurotechnology, Eleanor resisted. She did not want to feel monitored. Eventually, she agreed—not for improvement, but for continuity. The system was gentle. It tracked her cognitive rhythms, suggested mental exercises, and adjusted her daily routine subtly. There were no alarms, no corrections. Just guidance.

Over months, Eleanor noticed fewer blank moments. Not perfection—just steadiness. The words returned more easily. She resumed writing longer entries, reflecting not only on her past, but on the present. The technology did not stop aging. It slowed the confusion enough for meaning to remain accessible.

One afternoon, Eleanor forgot to charge the device. The day felt heavier. Thoughts scattered. She grew frustrated, then paused. She opened her notebook and wrote anyway, slowly.

The process was harder, but possible. When the system resumed the next day, Eleanor felt gratitude—but also pride. The support had helped her practice resilience, not avoid difficulty. As years passed, Eleanor's writing changed. Fewer details, more essence. The AI adapted, prioritizing emotional clarity over precision. Her daughter read the notebooks later and found not decline, but evolution. The voice remained unmistakably Eleanor's.

Near the end of her life, Eleanor wrote one final line: *I am still here*. The technology had not preserved her youth. It had preserved her presence. And in that presence, her words lived on—clear enough, long enough, to be remembered.

Chapter 10

The Future of the AI-Connected Mind

After exploring restoration, decoding, feedback loops, augmentation, ethics, symbiosis, limits, consciousness, and longevity, one question remains unavoidable: where is this all leading? The future of the AI-connected mind is not a single invention or endpoint, but a gradual transformation in how humans relate to intelligence, learning, and self-development. This chapter examines that future not as science fiction, but as an extension of trends already underway, shaped by biological reality, ethical choice, and human intention.

The most significant shift ahead is not technological, but conceptual. Intelligence will no longer be defined solely by internal brain capacity or external tools, but by the quality of interaction between the two. AI-connected minds will learn faster, regulate more efficiently, and adapt more gracefully—but only if systems are designed to complement human cognition rather than override it. The future favors partnership, not replacement. Brain–AI integration becomes an interface for growth rather than a shortcut to dominance.

One emerging frontier is predictive neurotechnology. As AI models accumulate longitudinal neural data, they will increasingly anticipate cognitive needs rather than respond reactively. Fatigue, stress overload, attentional collapse, and emotional dysregulation may be identified hours or days in advance. This does not imply control, but preparedness. The mind gains foresight about itself. When combined with user consent and transparency, predictive support can prevent burnout, accelerate recovery, and preserve long-term cognitive health.

Another future direction lies in adaptive identity scaffolding. As individuals move through life stages—education, career intensity, caregiving, aging—their cognitive priorities shift. AI neurotechnology will increasingly adjust its role accordingly, offering challenge when growth is desired and stability when preservation is needed. This adaptability distinguishes humane systems from rigid optimization engines. The future mind is not perpetually maximized; it is contextually supported.

Neural interfaces may also become more ambient and less intrusive. Rather than explicit sessions or visible devices, future neurotech may blend into environments—lighting, sound, pacing, and interaction patterns that respond to cognitive states without demanding attention. In this model, technology disappears into experience. The brain benefits without being constantly reminded of the tool. This invisibility is not loss of control, but maturation of design.

Speculation often turns toward extreme outcomes: mind uploading, digital immortality, or fully merged consciousness. Chapter 10 addresses these ideas cautiously. While AI may increasingly model cognitive patterns, subjective experience remains embodied and context-dependent. The self is not a dataset that can be copied intact. Future neurotechnology is more likely to extend continuity of experience than to duplicate it. The goal is not eternal replication, but meaningful presence across time.

Education will be transformed by AI-connected minds. Learning may become less about memorization and more about pattern recognition, integration, and creative synthesis. Neurotechnology can help students understand how they learn, not just what they learn. This self-knowledge accelerates mastery and reduces frustration. However, this future demands ethical restraint. Education must cultivate curiosity and agency, not dependency on feedback systems.

Societal implications will depend on governance choices made early. If access to neurotechnology remains limited, cognitive inequality may widen. If access is broad and ethically guided, societies may benefit from greater mental resilience, reduced burnout, and extended productive engagement across lifespans. The technology itself does not determine outcomes. Policy, culture, and values do.

Chapter 10 emphasizes that the future of the AI-connected mind is not inevitable—it is participatory. Each design decision, regulatory framework, and individual choice shapes how integration unfolds. Neurotechnology amplifies intention. When aligned with human well-being, it becomes a tool for flourishing. When misaligned, it risks alienation. The responsibility is collective.

This chapter concludes with a reframing of "Human 2.0." This is not a superior species or an optimized brain, but a more self-aware one. A human who understands attention, regulates emotion, adapts to change, and uses technology consciously rather than compulsively. AI does not create this evolution. It supports it. The future mind remains human—more informed, more resilient, and more capable of choosing how it grows.

The Inheritance of Thought

Leo grew up in a world where cognitive support was normal. His grandmother had used early neurotechnology to preserve memory in her final years. His parents used it selectively, balancing demanding careers with mental health. By the time

Leo reached adulthood, the technology felt neither novel nor intimidating. It was simply an option.

As a systems designer, Leo worked on next-generation adaptive neurointerfaces. Yet he was cautious in his own use. He remembered his grandmother's notebooks, his father's deliberate pauses, his mother's insistence on rest. The technology had helped them—but it had not lived their lives for them. That distinction mattered.

One evening, while reviewing a prototype, Leo noticed the system recommending increasingly aggressive optimization. The metrics looked impressive. Engagement up. Fatigue delayed. Productivity sustained. Still, something felt wrong. The system had no concept of satisfaction—only continuation.

Leo rewrote the parameters. He introduced decay, silence, intentional inefficiency. The system resisted at first, then adapted. Performance dipped slightly. User reports improved. People felt better, not just sharper.

Years later, Leo taught a seminar on cognitive design. A student asked whether the future would involve constant neural enhancement. Leo paused, then told a story about his grandmother writing *I am still here.* He explained that the future of intelligence was not endless amplification, but preservation of meaning.

That night, Leo disabled his own interface and sat quietly. His mind wandered. Ideas surfaced slowly. He smiled. The technology would be there tomorrow. Tonight, he wanted to remember why it existed.

The inheritance of thought, Leo believed, was not code or hardware. It was discernment—the ability to use tools without surrendering the self. In that balance, the future of the AI-connected mind quietly took shape.

Epilogue

The Mind, Remembered

This book has traveled from the earliest experiments in brain–computer interfaces to the furthest horizons of the AI-connected mind. Along the way, it has examined recovery, decoding, feedback, augmentation, ethics, limits, consciousness, longevity, and future evolution. The epilogue is not a summary, but a distillation—an opportunity to step back from mechanisms and possibilities and ask what truly remains when the technology quiets. In the end, neurotechnology is not the story. The human mind is.

One of the clearest lessons across every chapter is that the brain does not want to be controlled. It wants to be understood. AI succeeds in neurotechnology not by overpowering cognition, but by listening to it carefully and responding with restraint. When systems fail, they fail by demanding too much—too much optimization, too much intervention, too much certainty. When they succeed, they do so quietly, fading into the background as the brain relearns its own balance. The future of brain–AI integration will be shaped not by ambition alone, but by humility.

Throughout this journey, a pattern emerges: the most meaningful benefits of neurotechnology occur when users internalize what the system reveals. Whether restoring movement, sharpening focus, regulating emotion, or preserving memory, AI acts as a mirror. It reflects the brain's states, rhythms, and capacities back to itself. Once that reflection is understood, the mirror can be set aside. The brain retains the skill. This is not dependence—it is education at the level of neural experience.

The epilogue also reinforces a crucial boundary. Intelligence, awareness, and identity are not outputs to be engineered. They are processes to be supported. Neurotechnology does not create presence, purpose, or meaning. It creates conditions in which those qualities are easier to access. This distinction protects the integrity of the human experience. A tool that claims to manufacture meaning will always fail. A tool that clears noise so meaning can emerge may endure.

Ethics, revisited here, is not a constraint on progress but its compass. The closer technology moves to the mind, the more important consent, agency, and reversibility become. The right to disengage, to choose effort over ease, to accept imperfection—these are not inefficiencies. They are expressions of humanity. Any future in which brain–AI integration thrives will be one that preserves these choices rather than erasing them. Another enduring insight is that neurotechnology reveals how adaptive the brain truly is. Even late in life, even after injury, even under chronic stress, the brain remains capable of reorganization when given clear feedback and appropriate challenge. AI does not grant this capacity; it illuminates it. In doing so, it changes the narrative of limitation into one of responsiveness. This reframing alone may be one of the greatest gifts of the field.

As you close this book, it is worth remembering that the most advanced interface is not silicon or code, but attention. Where attention is placed, the brain follows. AI can guide attention, but it cannot replace the choice to attend. The future of the AI-connected mind will depend less on breakthroughs and more on how intentionally these tools are used. Progress will be measured not only by capability, but by wisdom.

The epilogue leaves you with a simple but demanding idea: technology should make us more available to life, not less. More present, not more distracted. More capable of listening—to others, to the world, and to our own inner signals. When neurotechnology fulfills this role, it becomes an ally of consciousness rather than a competitor.

In the end, the question is not how far the mind can be extended, but how well it can be inhabited. AI may help us see the mind more clearly, protect it more gently, and support it more intelligently. But the act of being human—of noticing, choosing, remembering—remains irreducibly ours. That is not a limitation. It is the point.

When the Lights Went Out

The city lost power just before sunset. Screens dimmed, systems paused, and the quiet arrived faster than anyone expected. For most people, the interruption was inconvenient. For Daniel, it was unfamiliar. He had lived the last decade with subtle neural assistance—ambient adjustments to focus, emotional regulation cues, cognitive pacing woven into daily life. He rarely thought about it. Until it was gone.

At first, Daniel waited for the system to return. He checked his watch, then his phone, then laughed at himself. None of it worked. He sat on his balcony as the sky darkened naturally, without calibrated lighting or adaptive filters. His thoughts felt slower, less organized. He noticed impatience rising, then settling. There was no feedback to guide him—only sensation.

As the evening deepened, Daniel felt something unexpected: curiosity. Without prompts or optimization, his mind wandered freely. Memories surfaced without categorization. Ideas connected loosely, imperfectly. He realized how much of his mental life had become efficient—and how little of it had been allowed to meander. Neighbors emerged onto balconies and sidewalks. Conversations started, unfiltered by schedules or alerts. Daniel listened more than he spoke. Without neural cues to manage engagement, he relied on instinct. It was clumsy at first, then natural. The absence of assistance sharpened his awareness of effort, but also of choice.

Hours later, when the power returned, Daniel did not rush inside. He watched the city reawaken, lights blinking on, systems resuming their silent work. His interface reconnected automatically, ready to smooth cognition and restore pace. He hesitated, then adjusted it to its lowest setting.

That night, Daniel wrote in a notebook—by hand. He did not write about optimization or performance. He wrote about noticing the wind, the rhythm of conversation, the way his mind felt when left alone long enough to remember itself. The technology had supported him well. But the outage had reminded him why it mattered.

In the weeks that followed, Daniel changed nothing dramatic. He still used neurotechnology. He still valued its support. What changed was his relationship to it. He allowed more silence. More friction. More unassisted thought. The system adapted, as it always did, to his intention.

Years later, Daniel would describe that evening not as a failure of infrastructure, but as a gift. When the lights went out, the mind remained. And in that quiet, he rediscovered something no interface could provide—his own presence, waiting patiently to be acknowledged.

www.ingramcontent.com/pod-product-compliance
Ingram Content Group UK Ltd.
Pitfield, Milton Keynes, MK11 3LW, UK
UKHW020155290926
15471UKWH00005B/892

9 798295 627378